a SAVOR THE SOUTH™ *cookbook*

Peaches

a SAVOR THE SOUTH™ *cookbook*

Peaches

KELLY ALEXANDER

The University of North Carolina Press CHAPEL HILL

The paper in this book meets the guidelines for permanence and durability of
the Committee on Production Guidelines for Book Longevity of the Council on
Library Resources. The University of North Carolina Press has been a member
of the Green Press Initiative since 2003.

Library of Congress Cataloging-in-Publication Data
Alexander, Kelly.
Peaches / Kelly Alexander.
pages cm. — (A savor the South cookbook)
Includes index.
ISBN 978-1-4696-0197-7 (cloth : alk. paper) 1. Cooking (Peaches) I. Title.
TX813.P4A44 2012
641.6′425—dc23   2012026668

17 16 15 14 13   5 4 3 2 1

To my sister, friend,
and fellow native Georgian,
Laura Sheffield Bennett

*Life is better than death, I believe,
if only because it is less boring and because it has
fresh peaches in it.* —ALICE WALKER

Contents

a SAVOR THE SOUTH™ *cookbook*

Peaches

Introduction

MY FUZZY MEMORY

The single most memorable peach-flavored thing I ever ate was at a Fourth of July barbecue. I was twelve or thirteen years old, and I was with my friend Jamie's family. Jamie's parents were divorced, and her father had remarried. His new wife's relatives had a farm in North Georgia near the base of the Appalachian Trail, and it had a creek with a tire swing and a barn with chickens and roosters. Jamie's stepmother used to hand us fresh limes with peppermint sticks stuck in them like straws and tell us to go for a walk. I loved going with Jamie there. To a girl whose Jewish grandparents settled in Atlanta by way of the Bronx—I knew more about chopped liver than I did about creamed corn—the rural setting was marvelously exotic.

The barbecue featured a whole hog with an apple in its mouth that was roasting on a spit over a homemade open fire pit. This was my first pig-pickin', and it was a textbook example of the genre. Jamie's stepcousins were square dancing and creek-stomping, and there was a buffet table stocked with smoked meats, cornbread, potato salad, and just about every other iconic food of the American South you can conjure. Alongside the red-white-and-blue Jell-O mold and other tempting sweets, the dessert table contained small buckets of peaches, a gigantic deep-dish peach pie, and old-fashioned wooden churns, the dark and heavy barrel-like kind you pour rock salt into, filled with fresh peach ice cream.

It was this last dish that captured my attention—the peach ice cream. By that point in my life, I had consumed peach ice cream countless times, most of it the Mayfield brand, made with milk from a dairy that was founded in 1910 in Athens, Tennessee. To this day, Mayfield is distributed exclusively in the southeastern United States; after entering the Atlanta market in 1977, it almost immediately became the best-selling brand and has remained so

1

to this day. (In 1981, *Time* magazine named Mayfield the World's Best Ice Cream.) But back to the barbecue in question, which took place on a very, very hot day.

People from the South feel about the heat the way people from Chicago (and I should know because my husband is one of the latter) feel about the cold: proud. It may not make a lot of sense to let extreme weather become a source of regional pride, but when your weather is extreme, that's exactly what happens. You can always spot a real southerner on a hot day: We're the ones foolhardy enough to still be outside when the thermometer rises above 100°.

And so it was on the afternoon of the barbecue in question. Steam was rising all around the wooden churns, little wisps of cold white air shrouding the ice cream so that it looked like a mirage, like buckets of manna. When I finally bellied up to the table and scooped some out into my little paper bowl, it looked different from the peach ice cream I'd had before. I was used to ice cream that was peach-colored and smooth, a homogenized, factory-made product. What I was looking at, however, was goldenrod-yellow and studded with orange squares. When I sampled this strange concoction, I discovered that it wasn't so much peach-flavored as intensely cold custard loaded with fresh ripe peaches.

I stood in that large open field, in the days when a tick bite wasn't something that you worried could end your life, when I hadn't yet felt a proper kiss, when the Fourth of July seemed like it lasted for about a week squished into one perfect day . . . and that homemade peach ice cream was the most delicious thing I'd ever tasted. There is not a summer or a peach or a Fourth of July when I don't think about it, when I can't close my eyes and teleport back to that farm, to the hot sun on my face and the cold, creamy peach ice cream on my tongue. And that was the beginning of my relationship with the peach.

The assumption about women from Georgia is not just that we enjoy our celebrated native stone fruit, it's that we embody it. "Georgia peaches" means us girls born in the thirteenth of the original thirteen New World colonies, us girls who've rafted the Chattahoochee River, witnessed the Pink Floyd Laser Light

Show projected onto Stone Mountain, drunk Coca-Cola out of the bottle with boiled peanuts on the side. That's a Georgia peach for you.

I was born in Georgia and so was my mother, and being a girl from Georgia is a big part of who I am. It's why I'm soft on the outside but tough on the inside, rather like that peach for which the state is so well known. The only problem was that for a long time I carried a secret inside my summer tan (which was never protected well enough by sunscreen from the Georgia sun—another trait of the Georgia woman, I'm afraid, is sun addiction): For most of my early life, I didn't much care about peaches. It wasn't that I didn't appreciate their essence—sweet, floral, fragrant, summer in a fruit and all the rest. It was that they were so ubiquitous. There was fresh peach ice cream at *every* Fourth of July barbecue; there were peaches at *every* roadside stand when we drove to Florida; my grandfather ate a bowl of peaches topped with sour cream *every* day for breakfast (when it wasn't peach season, he went with canned).

You see, I may love being *from* Georgia, but I didn't always love being *in* Georgia. Growing up, I longed for the big city, the bustle and traffic and different sorts of people and different types of music. And when I got to New York City, I immediately noticed that girls all ate cut-up fruit that they bought from the refrigerated shelves of corner bodegas. A fresh peach was so rural, so rustic; a plastic container of perfectly diced pineapple or mango was so much more worldly and sophisticated. The city peaches were in your muffin or your plastic container of yogurt or the chutney at the Indian restaurant, never in the palm of your hand.

And a funny thing happened to me, the kind of thing that happens when you're far away from home and kind of blue and you go to a party and the Allman Brothers' song "Melissa" is playing and you remember that the Allman Brothers lived in Macon, Georgia, and that they had an album called *Eat a Peach*. ("Crossroads, will you ever let him go? Lord, Lord. / Or will you hide the dead man's ghost? / Or will he lie beneath the clay? / Or will his spirit float away? / But I know that he won't stay / without Melissa.") And then you want a peach more than you've ever wanted anything. You want to push your lips against that fuzzy skin, let your jaws go to work feasting on the flesh as the juice pours down your throat, let your teeth scrape the red pit to get every last bite. If this sounds like purple prose to you, I am not sorry: No edible flesh is more similar to human flesh than the peach's, and no skin or peel is as smooth as the one the peach wears. A peach's erotic properties are something we all must contend with, so why not celebrate them?

And you realize that a peach is Georgia and that Georgia is you and that the things that seem so common, so humble, are the things that make up your life. That's a Georgia peach.

Peach Basics: History, Varieties, and Tips for Choosing and Enjoying Peaches

The first thing to know about a peach is that it's a drupe, or a hard-stone fruit, and like its cousins the apricot and the plum, it's a member of the botanical family Rosaceae, which includes the rose. Despite the peach's seemingly eternal association with the American South, the fruit was actually first discovered more than 3,000 years ago growing wild in China, where it still grows freely and abundantly today.

Scientists and historians speculate that the peach tree has been cultivated since at least the tenth century. Because peach trees happen to be very adaptable to temperate climates, their spread from China westward through Kashmir and Persia was both fast and wildly successful—to the point that botanists initially believed that peaches were a native Persian fruit (their species name, in fact, is *persica*).

The noted food scholar Alan Davidson posits in his *Oxford Companion to Food* that, based on his research, "it is widely assumed that it was Alexander the Great who brought [the peach] to Greece from Persia." Regardless of who brought it, the peach got to Europe unharmed, and by the first century, the Romans had discovered its charms and began cultivating the fruit throughout their empire. Over time, peaches became especially esteemed in England and were popular with royalty both there and in France and the Netherlands. (China remains the world's largest peach producer; Italy and Greece are usually in the top five, too.) Eventually the Spaniards brought the fruit to the New World in the sixteenth century, introducing it to Saint Augustine, Florida, in 1513.

And that's when peaches began their long, complicated, and some say downright co-dependent relationship with the American South. The fruit and the southeastern U.S. climate are not necessarily an ideal match. California has cooler, more Mediterranean-like weather, and consequently it produces more peaches than any other state in the union—fully half of the American peach crop comes from there. But peaches obviously like life in the South because they've always grown here, too. Commercial production of the peach began to reach southward in earnest by the early nineteenth century, taking hold in what was then known as the "Chesapeake peach belt" on the Mid-Atlantic seaboard from southern New Jersey through Delaware and into Maryland.

When the peach hit Georgia and South Carolina, lightning struck. Although peaches had been growing in the state for a couple of hundred years, one cultivar of the fruit took the world by storm. First planted around 1870 on a farm in Macon County in middle Georgia, the Elberta peach, named for peach farmer Sam Rumph's wife, was the product of a Chinese tree grafted onto a local Georgia variety. The Elberta proved a remarkable advance for peaches in this country, a truly superior fruit that came from a combination of ancient and modern farming ingenuity. A large, firm, juicy peach with yellow rose-blushed flesh and a rich, creamy, buttery flavor, the Elberta was by the end of the century this country's top money-making peach, almost singularly funding the Georgia Southern railway lines as the peaches traveled from Georgia to large eastern cities.

But peaches, for all their glory, have a distinctively ephemeral nature. Most important, peach trees live only ten to twenty years at most. This means that a popular cultivar today may be eclipsed by newer, juicier, and more flavorful varieties within its lifetime and be unheard of fifteen years from now. (The Elberta, the ubiquitous fruit of my childhood, is now a "threatened" variety; because it's not frost-resistant, it never truly adapted to the

California climate and soil—which is necessary for a peach's survival in today's global produce marketplace.) New varieties come into the world and capture our collective palates with great regularity. There are the Haven peaches from Michigan (Halehaven, Sunhaven, Redhaven, Fairhaven, and others), developed by a horticulturalist at Michigan State University in the 1940s; the so-called "V" peaches of Ontario (Valiant, Velvet, Vedette, Veteran, and others), developed by the Horticultural Experiment Station in Vineland.

The important thing to know is that for more than 100 years, since Georgia first began shipping peaches beyond its borders, the state has claimed the fruit as its own. Georgia peach farmers believe that Georgia peaches offer a distinctive richness of flavor that comes from the state's particular combination of intense heat and red clay soil. South Carolina peaches are widely celebrated, but even though South Carolina overtook Georgia in peach production in the early 1950s, its peaches are somewhat lesser known. This is easy to understand when you consider that the state of Georgia features an image of the peach on its license plate, the Georgia quarter has a peach on its "tails" side, and more than fifty streets in Atlanta have the word "Peachtree" in their name.

When it comes to eating peaches, there are two general kinds: clingstone and freestone. Early-season peaches are cling or semi-cling; late-season peaches are freestone. Both clingstone and freestone, which are just terms used to describe how tightly the peach flesh adheres to the pit, include yellow-fleshed and white-fleshed varieties. Almost all fresh peaches sold in groceries and markets are freestone. They are softer and juicier, and since the pits pull away from the flesh easily, they can be cut into uniform pieces and are used widely in baking, especially in tarts or pies. Cling peaches are used mostly for canning and work best in recipes calling for diced or puréed peaches.

Some peach varieties are ancient, and some have been very recently cultivated. The range is vast and fairly amazing, comprising a family of beguilingly delicious—and very differently flavored and textured—fruits. Two of the world's most famous and well-established peach varieties are Admirable tardive and Grosse Noire de Montreuil, both of which come from the town of Montreuil near Paris, where peaches have been specially cultivated for hundreds of years. They are prized for their fine, clear skins (and, like most French peach varieties, are almost never seen in the United States). But new varieties of peaches seem to come out every summer. More than forty varieties of peaches are currently grown in South Carolina.

No matter where they're from, peaches are good for you. A medium peach has about 38 calories (they're nearly 90 percent water) and a load of nutrients. They're especially high in vitamins A and C, potassium, and fiber.

There are a few essential things to know when choosing peaches. White peaches tend to be lower in acidity than yellow ones, so plan accordingly for recipes. For cooking and baking, freestones are easier to work with and usually a better choice. The most important tool you have for choosing a good peach is your hands: Look for peaches that give just slightly when pressed and are neither rock-hard nor soft. The second most important tool is your eyes, which you should use to examine peaches for bruises or broken skin. Pick only intact, unbruised specimens. Also avoid peaches with traces of green around their stems, which indicate that they were picked too early and won't ripen nicely. Finally, you should choose peaches with your nose: Peaches should have a mild scent but should not be wildly fragrant (an indication of over-ripeness).

The single best way to enjoy a peach is after it has been allowed to ripen on the tree. Peaches that are shipped are often picked long before they ripen and tend to be rubbery, tasteless, mealy, and floury. These peaches give good peaches a bad name. That said, a fresh ripe peach is often so delicious that it's hard to recommend cooking one at all.

The ideal peach will be full of sweetness and juice and free of bruises. Peaches that fit this description, even at the height of the midsummer season, don't just grow on trees. Well, they do, but the perfect peach is elusive. You have to be there. The best bet for ripeness is to buy peaches at least a day or two before you plan to serve them. Unless you're shopping at the kind of place that will carefully cradle each peach in paper for you, handle them with care. All peaches, even the baseball-hard ones, are delicate and benefit from careful handling so as to avoid bruising. Try not to let them touch their neighbors, and try not to move or jostle them too much, either.

To more quickly ripen slightly green or firm peaches, place them at room temperature stem-side down in a paper bag with the top folded down. This will trap the gases and speed the ripening. In general, refrigerate peaches only after they've ripened, which can prolong freshness for up to five days. If you should come into a lot of very ripe peaches, refrigerate those that will not be eaten immediately to slow further ripening. Separate out peaches with large bruises or brown spots, which could quickly spread to the other peaches. Cut off the damaged flesh and immediately use the good sections in recipes.

The easiest way to peel peaches is to plunge them into boiling water for about twenty seconds, then immediately transfer them to ice-cold water to halt the heating process. Use a paring knife to gently pull off the skin, starting at the stem end. To keep the peeled peach flesh from turning brown, sprinkle it with fresh lemon juice.

"Do I dare to eat a peach?" is the question that the narrator in T. S. Eliot's famous poem "The Love Song of J. Alfred Prufrock" asks himself. Here the peach represents the subject's fears and anxieties about his existence: Will he cease contemplating and analyzing his life and start living it? Will he taste the ripeness not only of his time on earth but also of his ladylove? Will he allow himself to fully live in the moment instead of wringing his hands in regret? In literature, art, and life, the peach is a powerful symbol, but more than anything, it's delicious—nature's candy, if you will. We should all dare to eat a peach as often as we're able.

Desserts

Is it unorthodox to begin a cookbook with dessert recipes? Definitely . . . if the subject of the book is one other than peaches. If you're going to transform a peach by cooking it, the most obvious thing it could become is something sweet. And so it's fitting, in this case, to begin where a meal usually ends—with ice cream, cake, pie, and other such treats—because these are the foods we most associate with peaches. All our lives we've been taught that we must earn our desserts, but in the case of the noble peach, dessert comes first.

The Best Peach Ice Cream

In this day of fat-free frozen yogurt, it's hard to remember how real peach ice cream should taste: impossibly rich, custardy, and spiked with a hint of intensely sweet peach flavor and aroma. It's so luscious that one small bowl of it is worth gallons of fat-free frozen peach yogurt. It's possible to prepare the mixture for this ice cream in fifteen minutes.

MAKES 1 GENEROUS QUART

3 large egg yolks
¾ cup packed light brown sugar
1½ cups heavy cream
1½ cups whole milk
2 tablespoons lemon juice
1 teaspoon vanilla
1 vanilla bean (optional)
3 large peaches, peeled, pitted, and cut into bite-size chunks

In a large bowl, whisk together the egg yolks and brown sugar. In a large saucepan, bring the cream and milk to a simmer over low heat. Whisking constantly, slowly pour the hot milk mixture into the egg yolk mixture until combined; return to the saucepan. Cook over low heat, stirring constantly, for 3–5 minutes or until the custard has thickened enough to coat the back of a spoon. Immediately strain the custard into a bowl. Set the bowl in a larger bowl filled with ice water to cool, stirring occasionally.

When the custard has cooled, stir in the lemon juice, vanilla, and vanilla bean, if desired. Chill overnight. Remove the vanilla bean and freeze in an ice cream maker according to the manufacturer's instructions, adding the peaches halfway through the churning process.

VARIATION ❋ The Atlanta-based Food Network chef Alton Brown knows a thing a two about kitchen science (the technical aspect of recipes is the focus of his shows). His ingenious recipe for Burnt Peach Ice Cream relies on the flavor of golden brown caramelized peaches. This ice cream has a deep sweetness and a chunkier texture than regular peach ice cream.

To caramelize the peaches, heat the oven to 400°. In a 9 × 13-inch baking dish, combine 3 tablespoons unsalted butter, ⅔ cup sugar, and ¼ cup water. Place the dish in the oven until the butter melts. Remove from the oven and stir to combine. Cut each peach in half and remove the pits. Arrange the peach halves in the dish cut-side down. Roast until the peaches are tender, about 20 minutes. If desired, slip the peach skins off and discard. Chop the peaches roughly.

Combine all ingredients in the recipe above (including the bean and its pulp) except the peaches in a large saucepan and place over medium heat. Stirring occasionally, bring just barely to a simmer. As soon as you see a bubble on the surface, remove the custard from the heat and strain it into a lidded container. Cool completely, then refrigerate overnight to mellow the flavors and solidify the texture.

Freeze the custard in an ice cream maker according to the manufacturer's instructions. The ice cream will not freeze hard in the machine; it will still be sludgy. Once the volume has increased by half and reached a soft-serve consistency, add the peaches and continue churning to incorporate. Spoon the ice cream back into a lidded container and harden completely in the freezer for at least 1 hour before serving.

Caroline and David's Peach Frozen Yogurt

The writers and editors I worked with during my time at Saveur *form a particularly close-knit professional tribe. Caroline Campion is among these folks, although she worked at the magazine after I left. When she recommended I buy the book* Perfect Scoop *by David Lebovitz, who made the desserts for years at Berkeley's famed Chez Panisse restaurant, I asked her what was so special about it. Caroline gave as an example his recipe for peach frozen yogurt. Before I had time to buy the book, I ended up getting the recipe from Caroline, so this is really a secondhand recipe. Caroline says, "The color is so beautiful—a soft pinkish coral—you can't believe it's real, and the taste is just extraordinary."*

MAKES 1 PINT

1½ pounds very ripe peaches, peeled, pitted, and cut into chunks
½ cup water
¾ cup sugar
1 cup Greek yogurt
Lemon juice

In a medium saucepan over medium heat, cook the peaches in the water, covered, stirring occasionally, until soft and cooked through, about 10 minutes. Remove the peaches from the heat, stir in the sugar, then chill completely in the refrigerator, about 1 hour.

When the peaches are chilled, purée them with any remaining liquid in a blender with the yogurt until smooth (if you like chunky frozen yogurt, leave some chunks). Mix in a few drops of lemon juice. Freeze the mixture in your ice cream maker according to the manufacturer's directions.

Peaches and Bourbon Cream

Peaches-and-cream is, at its best, exactly what it sounds like. You can certainly make it by pouring a little cream over fresh peaches, and it will be great. But if you chill the glasses, spike the cream with bourbon, and garnish the dessert with slivered almonds, it will be ethereal. This dessert is a validation of attention to detail!

MAKES 4 SERVINGS

---

4 peaches, sliced ¼-inch thick
2 tablespoons light brown sugar, divided
1 teaspoon vanilla
1 cup heavy cream
4 teaspoons bourbon
Toasted slivered almonds

At least 1 hour but no more than 4 hours before serving, refrigerate 4 dessert glasses or bowls.

In a large nonreactive bowl, combine the peaches with 1 tablespoon of the brown sugar and the vanilla. Cover with plastic wrap and set aside until the peach juices run and most of the sugar dissolves, about 1 hour.

In a medium bowl, whip the cream until it thickens and soft peaks form, and then beat in the remaining 1 tablespoon of brown sugar. Add the bourbon and continue beating until soft peaks form. Layer the peaches and whipped cream in the chilled dessert glasses or bowls. Serve immediately, sprinkled with toasted slivered almonds.

Perfect Peach Pie

If you close your eyes and imagine a perfect peach pie, it will be this one: buttery, rich, and almost completely reliant on the quality of the fruit for its appeal. That said, this recipe is also a blank canvas waiting to be personalized. To the filling, you could add a little freshly ground cinnamon for warmth, some torn basil for an edgy sweetness and aroma, or a few drops of almond essence. To the crust, you could add some pulverized almonds. Whatever you decide, this recipe is an ideal jumping-off point, but it's also mighty fine the way it is.

MAKES 1 9-INCH PIE

FOR THE CRUST

2⅔ cups all-purpose flour
2 teaspoons sugar
¾ teaspoon salt
1 stick cold unsalted butter, cut into ½-inch pieces
½ cup plus 1 tablespoon cold vegetable shortening
½ cup ice water

FOR THE FILLING

8 large peaches
¾ cup sugar
1½ tablespoons lemon juice
¼ cup plus 1 tablespoon all-purpose flour
1½ tablespoons unsalted butter, thinly sliced
Egg wash made with 1 large egg yolk mixed with
    2 tablespoons water

In a food processor, pulse the flour with the sugar and salt until combined. Add the butter and shortening and pulse until the mixture resembles coarse meal. Transfer the mixture to a large bowl and sprinkle the ice water on top. Stir with a fork until a crumbly dough forms. Turn the dough out onto a work surface and knead 2 or 3 times, just until the dough comes together. Cut the dough in half and form 2 disks; cover in plastic wrap and refrigerate until firm, at least 30 minutes or overnight.

On a lightly floured surface, roll out each disk to a 12-inch round. Ease one of the rounds into a 9-inch glass pie plate and transfer the other round to a baking sheet. Refrigerate.

Preheat the oven to 400°. Bring a large saucepan of water to a boil and fill a large bowl with ice water. Using a sharp knife, cut a shallow X in the bottom of each peach. Blanch the peaches in the boiling water for about 1 minute, until the skins begin to loosen. Using a slotted spoon, transfer the peaches to the ice water to cool. Drain and peel the peaches and cut them into ¾-inch wedges. Transfer the peaches to a large bowl. Add the sugar, lemon juice, and flour, toss well, and let stand for 5 minutes.

Pour the peaches and their juices into the chilled pie shell and scatter the butter slices on top. Brush the edge of the pie shell with the egg wash and lay the round of dough from the baking sheet on top. Press the edges of the pie shell together to seal and trim the overhang to ½ inch. Fold the edge of the pie dough under and crimp decoratively. Brush the remaining egg wash on the top crust and cut a few slits for venting steam.

Transfer the pie to the oven and place a baking sheet on the rack underneath to catch any drips. Bake for 30 minutes. Reduce the oven temperature to 375°, cover the edge of the crust with foil, and bake for about 40 minutes longer, until the filling is bubbling and the crust is deeply golden on the top and bottom. Transfer the pie to a rack to cool completely. Serve warm or at room temperature with vanilla ice cream or whipped cream if you like.

Individual Peach-Pecan Crisps

The interplay between the peach's natural sweetness and soft flesh and the rich, buttery nature and crunch of the pecan is indigenous southern fruit-and-nut fusion at its best. This crisp is an excellent and easy summer dinner-party dessert. If you don't have enough individual ovenproof dishes, this dessert can be made just as easily in your favorite medium-sized baking dish.

MAKES 6 SERVINGS

1 cup pecan halves

¼ cup plus 2 tablespoons all-purpose flour

¼ cup plus 2 tablespoons packed light brown sugar

½ cup plus 2 tablespoons granulated sugar, divided

6 tablespoons unsalted butter, cut into ½-inch dice

½ cup old-fashioned rolled oats

2½ pounds peaches, quartered, pitted, and sliced crosswise
   ¼-inch thick

½ cup dried sour cherries, blueberries, cranberries,
   or a combination

1 pint ice cream, preferably cinnamon, vanilla,
   or coffee flavored

Preheat the oven to 350°. Spread the pecans on a baking sheet and bake for 6–8 minutes or until lightly toasted. Let the nuts cool, then coarsely chop them. Leave the oven on.

In a food processor, pulse the flour with the brown sugar and ¼ cup of the granulated sugar until combined. Add the butter and pulse until the mixture resembles coarse meal. Transfer to a bowl and stir in the toasted pecans and oats.

Generously butter 6 individual baking dishes that are about 6 inches wide and 1 inch deep. In a medium bowl, toss the peaches with the dried fruit and the remaining 6 tablespoons of granulated sugar. Divide the peach mixture among the prepared baking dishes and cover with the topping. Set the dishes on a large baking sheet and bake in the bottom third of the oven for 45–50 minutes or until the peaches are tender when pierced and the topping is toasted. Serve warm with ice cream.

Fresh Peach Upside-Down Cake

According to food historians, the term "upside-down cake" first began appearing in recipes in the late 1800s. (Up until then, such desserts were called "skillet cakes"—this was long before ovens were commonplace in homes, so skillets had multiple uses.) The first upside-down cakes were made with seasonal fruits like apples and pears in the fall and cherries and peaches in the summer. But in 1925 the Hawaiian Pineapple Company, founded by James Dole (now the Dole Company), sponsored a contest calling for pineapple recipes. The company was reportedly flooded with pineapple upside-down cakes, and soon after, recipes for them began appearing in magazines, cookbooks, and advertisements. Pineapple became the "it" upside-down cake. The peach's distinctly nutty-sweet flavor and heady, flowery aroma lend the cake a more complex richness. If you don't have a cast-iron skillet, you can bake the cake in a greased 9-inch cake pan. Just be sure to make the butter-sugar mixture for the topping in a nonstick skillet so you can pour it into the prepared cake pan.

MAKES 8 SERVINGS

1½ sticks unsalted butter, at room temperature, divided

⅔ cup granulated sugar, divided

⅓ cup packed light brown sugar

1 pound peaches, peeled, pitted, and sliced ¾-inch thick

1¼ cups cake flour (not self-rising)

1 teaspoon baking powder

½ teaspoon cinnamon

¼ teaspoon grated nutmeg

¼ teaspoon salt

2 large eggs, at room temperature

⅓ cup milk

½ teaspoon almond extract

½ teaspoon vanilla

Preheat the oven to 350°. Melt ½ stick of the butter in a 9- or 10-inch cast-iron skillet over medium heat, using a brush to coat the sides of the skillet. Add ⅓ cup of the granulated sugar plus all the brown sugar and cook, stirring constantly, until the mixture bubbles and becomes creamy and smooth, about 2–3 minutes. Remove the skillet from the heat and gently push the peach slices into the soft caramel, arranging them in concentric circles. Set aside.

Mix the flour, baking powder, cinnamon, nutmeg, and salt in a medium bowl. In a large bowl, beat the remaining 1 stick of butter and remaining ⅓ cup of granulated sugar with a mixer on medium speed until pale and fluffy, about 3 minutes; beat in the eggs, one at a time, until blended. On low speed, beat in half of the flour mixture, the milk, the extracts, and then the remaining flour mixture until the batter is smooth.

Spoon the batter into the skillet, and using a spatula, gently spread it over the peaches in an even layer to the sides of the skillet. Bake for 35–40 minutes, until the top is golden brown and a tester inserted into the center of the cake comes out clean.

Let the cake cool in the skillet on a rack for 10 minutes. Run a sharp knife around the cake's edge, invert a serving plate over the top of the skillet, and, using oven mitts, turn out the cake onto the plate. Carefully replace any peach slices that might have stuck to the skillet. Serve the cake warm or at room temperature, with whipped cream or peach ice cream if you like.

Aromatic Red Wine–Poached Peaches

France produces some of the best peaches in the world, so it's not surprising that French chefs have come up with a great way to prepare them: gently poached in wine. This recipe is adapted from one by the legendary southern French chef Roger Vergé, a pioneer of modern haute French cooking. In his book New Entertaining in the French Style, *Vergé writes that when he was a child, his aunt used to poach peaches in red wine and add a generous glass of cassis to the syrup just before serving. As a kid, he wasn't permitted to eat the fruit, but he was allowed to taste the syrup. This recipe is clearly his revenge.*

MAKES 6 SERVINGS

1 cup port
Peel of ½ lemon
1 vanilla bean
6 bay leaves
½ bottle red wine such as Côte du Rhone or pinot noir
2–3 tablespoons honey
6 peaches

In a large saucepan, combine the port, lemon peel, vanilla bean, bay leaves, and wine and bring to a boil. Stir in the honey and remove the saucepan from the heat. Add more honey if necessary. Cover the saucepan and set aside.

Fill a large saucepan halfway with water and bring to a boil. Plunge the peaches into the boiling water for 2 minutes, then rinse them under cold water and peel them. Place them in the warm wine mixture over medium high heat and bring to a gentle simmer. Simmer gently for 10 minutes, taking care not to let the peaches boil. Remove from the heat, cover, and cool.

Remove the fruit from the syrup and place in a shallow bowl. Pick out the bay leaves and stick them in the peaches at the stem end where the leaves would be. Cut the vanilla bean into six segments and place one in each peach to make a stem. Serve warm or at room temperature.

North Carolina Barbecue Joint–Style Peach Cobbler

This fruit dessert is a staple at barbecue joints across the state, and its humble excellence is perhaps the one thing that folks who like eastern-style and folks who like western-style barbecue can agree upon. And it's true that most of these places have their own twist on the genre: Some use double-crust versions, and a great many rely on canned peaches even when the real ones are in season—nearly all employ a mixture of brown sugar and butter for the crust. That said, this recipe is as close to the genuine article you can get, and it's a very homespun—and fairly sweet—guilty pleasure.

MAKES 6 SERVINGS

---

3 cups peaches, skin-on or peeled, sliced 1/4-inch thick

1 cup plus 1 tablespoon granulated sugar, divided

1 tablespoon cornstarch

2 tablespoons water

2 cups all-purpose flour

1/2 cup lightly packed light brown sugar

1 stick unsalted butter, cut into small pieces

1 teaspoon cinnamon

Preheat the oven to 375°. Place the peach slices and ½ cup of the granulated sugar in a medium saucepan and bring to a boil over medium-high heat. Meanwhile, mix together the cornstarch and water in a small bowl, then add to the peaches and cook, stirring, for 1 minute. Transfer the peaches and thickened juices to an 8 × 8-inch baking dish and set aside.

Sift together the flour, ½ cup granulated sugar, and the brown sugar in a medium mixing bowl. Using a pastry cutter or two knives, work the butter into the flour until it resembles coarse meal. Spread the topping evenly over the peach filling and pat down firmly with the palms of your hands and your fingers, smoothing out the top. Sprinkle the topping with the remaining 1 tablespoon of granulated sugar and the cinnamon.

Bake the cobbler in the oven until the crust is golden brown and bubbly, about 40 minutes. Set aside to cool briefly before serving with whipped cream or ice cream if you like.

Peach Clafoutis

Clafoutis *is a classic French dessert with a thick, rich batter that is like a cross between a baked pancake and a sweet omelet. Although it's traditionally made with cherries (particularly the French variety called Montmorency), it's fun and easy to substitute peaches, which produce a sweeter result. The almond extract adds warmth and depth to the dessert's flavor.*

MAKES 6–8 SERVINGS

6 medium peaches
3 large eggs, at room temperature
1 cup milk
2 tablespoons melted unsalted butter
1 teaspoon vanilla
½ teaspoon almond extract (optional)
1 teaspoon salt
½ cup sugar
¾ cup all-purpose flour

Preheat the oven to 450°. Lightly grease a 9-inch round cake pan.

Bring a medium saucepan filled with water to a boil. Add the peaches and cook for 1–2 minutes, then drain. When the peaches are cool enough to handle, peel, pit, and slice each one into eighths. Scatter the peach slices evenly over the bottom of the prepared dish.

In a blender, mix the eggs, milk, butter, vanilla, and almond extract, if desired, until frothy. Pour into a medium bowl. Whisk in the salt, sugar, and flour until combined.

Pour the batter over the peaches in the pan. Bake for 20 minutes, just until the top begins to puff up. Reduce the heat to 350° and bake for an additional 20 minutes or until the top is lightly browned and a cake tester inserted into the center comes out clean. The edges should pull away from the sides of the pan. Remove from the oven. Cool on a wire rack for 5 minutes. Serve warm or at room temperature, with whipped cream or ice cream if you like.

Peach Crème Brûlée

The fad of flavored crème brûlées—from mint julep to cappuccino—hit Manhattan around the time I first moved there in the early 1990s. A classicist who adores the flavor of real vanilla, scraped from a bean, I didn't see what was so wrong with the original and eschewed reinterpretations—with one exception: Peaches are a natural for this treatment. Think of Peach Crème Brûlée as a very dressed up version of peaches-and-cream and serve it on special occasions.

MAKES 4 SERVINGS

½ pound peaches, peeled, pitted, and chopped
1 ounce peach schnapps
¼ cup whole milk
1½ cups heavy cream
2 teaspoons vanilla
1 (1-inch) piece of fresh ginger, peeled and finely grated
¾ cup sugar, plus more for sprinkling, divided
4 large egg yolks

Preheat the oven to 325°. In a medium saucepan, combine the peaches and schnapps and simmer over medium heat until the peaches become soft and tender, about 5 minutes. Set aside to cool.

Place the peach-schnapps mixture in a blender and purée until smooth. Return the mixture to the saucepan and add the milk, heavy cream, vanilla, and ginger and ⅜ cup of the sugar. Bring to a boil over moderate heat.

In a medium nonreactive bowl, whisk the remaining ⅜ cup of sugar with the egg yolks. Slowly whisk in the heated milk mixture. Continue whisking until the mixture becomes smooth, creamy, and thick, about 6–7 minutes.

Strain through a fine sieve and divide evenly into 4 ramekins, then place in a large roasting pan. Pour enough warm water into the pan to come about ⅓ of the way up the sides of ramekins. Bake until set, approximately 40–45 minutes. Remove the pan from the oven and cool the ramekins completely while still in the water bath. Cover each with plastic wrap and refrigerate until thoroughly chilled and set, at least 4 hours or preferably overnight.

Working with one custard at a time, sprinkle a small amount of sugar on the surface of each, just enough to provide a thin layer on top. Then hold a small kitchen blowtorch so the flame is 2 inches above the surface. Direct the flame so the sugar melts and browns, about 2 minutes.

Refrigerate until the custards are firm but the topping is still brittle, at least 2 hours but no longer than 4 hours.

Peach-Blackberry Crumble

*In a classic case of opposites attracting, sweet and fragrant peaches
have a natural affinity for tart, pucker-inducing blackberries; the
two bring out the best in each other, with the acidity of the berries
balancing the lushness of the peaches. This simple, homey dessert
gets a lift from the zest of the fresh ginger and the crunch of toasted,
cinnamon-spiked oats. When combining summer fruits like these,
choose the best and ripest you can find.*

MAKES 4 SERVINGS

¼ cup plus 2 tablespoons packed light brown sugar, divided
¼ cup all-purpose flour
¼ cup rolled oats
½ teaspoon cinnamon
Pinch of salt
2 tablespoons unsalted butter, cut into small pieces
½ cup coarsely chopped pecans
4 large peaches
2 tablespoons lemon juice
1 tablespoon cornstarch
1 teaspoon peeled and finely grated fresh ginger
1 cup fresh blackberries

Preheat the oven to 400°. In a medium bowl, combine ¼ cup of the brown sugar with the flour, oats, cinnamon, and salt. Using your fingers or a pastry blender, work in the butter until the mixture resembles peas. Stir in the pecans.

Bring a medium saucepan filled with water to a boil. Using a small sharp knife, make a shallow X in the bottom of each peach. Add the peaches to the boiling water and blanch for about 30 seconds, then remove and refresh with cold water. Peel, pit, and slice the peaches.

In a large bowl, toss the peaches with the lemon juice, cornstarch, ginger, and remaining 2 tablespoons of brown sugar. Fold in half of the berries and spoon the fruit into a 1-quart baking dish. Sprinkle the crumbs over the fruit, top with the remaining berries, and bake for about 30 minutes or until the fruit mixture is bubbling and the top is golden.

Sour Cream Peach Cake

This is a moist and very simple cake, a great one to bake with a kitchen-curious kid, made slightly more elegant thanks to slices of fresh peaches sandwiched between its rich layers. It's an excellent finish to a backyard barbecue or a light summer lunch, but it can also be a decadent breakfast during peach season.

MAKES 8 SERVINGS

1 stick unsalted butter, at room temperature

1½ cups sugar, divided

3 large eggs

1 cup sour cream

1 teaspoon vanilla

2 cups all-purpose flour

1 teaspoon baking soda

1 teaspoon baking powder

½ teaspoon kosher salt

1 teaspoon cinnamon

3 large peaches, peeled, pitted, and sliced

Preheat the oven to 350°. Grease a 9-inch square baking pan.

In the bowl of a stand mixer fitted with the paddle attachment, cream the butter and 1 cup of the sugar for 3–5 minutes on medium-high speed until light and fluffy. With the mixer on low, add the eggs one at a time, then the sour cream and vanilla, and mix until the batter is smooth. In a separate bowl, sift together the flour, baking soda, baking powder, and salt. With the mixer on low, slowly add the dry ingredients to the batter and mix just until combined. In a small bowl, combine the remaining ½ cup of sugar and the cinnamon.

Spread half of the batter evenly in the pan. Top with half of the peaches, then sprinkle with two-thirds of the sugar mixture. Spread the remaining batter on top, arrange the remaining peaches on top of that, and sprinkle with the remaining sugar mixture.

Bake for 45–55 minutes, until a toothpick inserted in the center comes out clean. Transfer to a rack to cool for at least 20 minutes. Cut into squares and serve warm or at room temperature topped with whipped cream or a favorite ice cream if you like.

Classic Peach Melba

This most famous of all peach desserts was created by the legendary French chef Auguste Escoffier in 1893 to honor Dame Nellie Melba, the Australian soprano, during her visit to his restaurant in London's Savoy Hotel. Its particular genius is the combination of peaches with a sweet-tart raspberry sauce. When served over creamy vanilla ice cream, it's summer in a glass. When you make this dish, reserve the peach-poaching liquid—combined with prosecco or another sparkling wine, it makes a refreshing cocktail.

MAKES 4 SERVINGS

4 peaches
1 whole vanilla bean, split lengthwise
1 cup plus 4 teaspoons sugar, divided
1 pint vanilla ice cream, softened
1 cup fresh raspberries
½ teaspoon lemon juice

Bring a large pot of water to a simmer over high heat. Lower the peaches into the simmering water and blanch just long enough to loosen their skins, about 1 minute. Transfer the peaches with a slotted spoon to a bowl of ice water to cool, then peel, halve lengthwise, and discard the pits. Put the peach halves and vanilla bean halves into a wide dish and sprinkle with 1 cup of the sugar. Cover with plastic wrap and set aside until the peach juices run and most of the sugar dissolves, about 1 hour.

Bring 3 cups of water to a boil in a medium pot over high heat. Add the peaches and the sugary juices and vanilla bean halves, reduce the heat to medium, and poach, gently stirring occasionally, until the peaches are just soft when pierced, about 10 minutes. Remove the pot from the heat, partially cover, and set aside until the peaches are cool, about 1 hour. Transfer the pot to the refrigerator until the peaches are thoroughly chilled, about 3 hours.

Divide the ice cream between 4 wide dessert dishes or parfait glasses, using the back of a spoon to make a smooth, even layer in the bottom of each dish. Transfer the dishes to the freezer until the ice cream is solid, about 30 minutes. Meanwhile, purée the raspberries in a blender, then strain through a sieve into a bowl, pressing the purée through with a rubber spatula; discard the seeds. Add the remaining 4 teaspoons of sugar and the lemon juice to the purée, stirring until the sugar dissolves.

To serve, arrange 2 peach halves, cut-side down, in each dish on top of the ice cream. Spoon the raspberry sauce over the peaches. Serve immediately.

Fried Peach Pies

The first fried pie I ever ate was at The Varsity, Atlanta's prototypical beloved fast-food joint, which opened its doors in 1928. Fried peach pies still come in individual waxed paper bags at that restaurant to this day, and they are a singular guilty pleasure. That said, they're not made with fresh peaches. This version retains the kitschy fun while maximizing the peach flavor.

MAKES 6 SERVINGS

1 stick plus 1 tablespoon unsalted butter, at room
    temperature, divided
3 tablespoons sugar, divided
1/4 teaspoon salt
1 large egg
1 1/2 cups all-purpose flour
2 tablespoons ice water
2 cups thinly sliced peaches
1/4 cup peach jam or preserves
Vegetable oil for frying

Beat together 1 stick of the butter, 2½ tablespoons of the sugar, and the salt for 3 minutes on medium speed in the bowl of a stand mixer. Add the egg and beat for 30 seconds. Add the flour and water and beat for 15 seconds. Turn off the machine, scrape down the sides of the bowl, and beat again for 10 seconds. Scoop out the dough with your hands and form it into a 1-inch-thick disk. Cover in plastic wrap and refrigerate for at least 1 hour.

Melt the remaining 1 tablespoon of butter over medium-high heat in a medium-sized pan. Sauté the peaches and remaining ½ tablespoon sugar until the sugar is dissolved, about 2 minutes. Add the jam or preserves and cook, stirring constantly, for 3 minutes, until the peaches soften and the jam melts. Remove from the heat and set aside to cool.

On a lightly floured surface, roll out the dough into a 16 × 11-inch rectangle about ⅛-inch thick. Cut out 6 circles 5¼ inches in diameter. (For a more free-form shape, divide the dough into 6 pieces and roll out.) Place the circles on a baking sheet lined with parchment or wax paper. Spread about ¼ cup of the cooled cooked peaches on half of each circle. Fold the other half over the filling and crimp the edges securely with a fork. Refrigerate for 20 minutes before frying.

Pour 2½ inches of oil into a heavy 4-quart saucepan or cast-iron skillet and heat to 350°. Fry the pies two or three at a time for 1½–2 minutes per batch or until golden brown. Drain on paper towels. Keep warm in a 200° oven until all the pies are fried. Serve immediately topped with ice cream if you like.

Easy Peachy Shortcakes

The word "shortcake" can conjure up many different images, from sponge and pound cakes to angel food cake. What makes a shortcake unique is that it's made with lots of shortening or butter. This is an authentic biscuit-style southern shortcake recipe, which means the shortcake is flaky and buttery — an excellent and not-too-sweet foil for the juicy peach's flavor. You can blanch the peaches in boiling water to remove the skins if you like, but it's not necessary.

MAKES 8 SERVINGS

½ pound small peaches, skin-on or peeled,
   cut into ½-inch chunks
1 tablespoon lemon juice
¼ cup plus 2 teaspoons sugar, plus more for sprinkling,
   divided
2 cups all-purpose flour, plus more for the work surface
1 tablespoon baking powder
½ teaspoon kosher salt
6 tablespoons unsalted butter, cut into small pieces
1 cup heavy cream, plus more for brushing

Preheat the oven to 400°. Combine the peaches and lemon juice and 2 teaspoons of the sugar. Let stand for 15 minutes.

Whisk together the flour, baking powder, salt, and remaining ¼ cup of sugar in a large bowl. Using a pastry blender, cut in the butter until the mixture forms small pieces. Stir in the cream. Fold in the peach mixture.

Turn out the dough onto a lightly floured surface and pat into an 8½-inch round. Using a 2½-inch cutter, cut out 8 rounds, then transfer each one to a parchment-lined baking sheet. Brush with cream; sprinkle with sugar. Bake until golden brown, 20–25 minutes. Let cool on a wire rack. Serve warm or at room temperature.

Breakfast

Nothing beats a fresh ripe peach for breakfast. My physician, Anna White, a native North Carolinian who loves peaches more than anyone I've ever known, often regales me with tales of her summer morning trips to the Raleigh Farmers' Market. Every Saturday during peach season, she buys a bushel of peaches, lugs it home to Chapel Hill, and then eats peach after peach over her kitchen sink for breakfast until they're gone. If you are lucky enough to have access to mouthwatering peaches, I suggest you do the same. And if you're feeling ambitious, there are some delicious ways to enjoy peaches in the morning that involve cooking. No day that begins with a taste of peach can turn out too badly—a peach-accented breakfast is a little like getting to eat dessert first thing in the morning.

Peach-Banana Smoothie

Like a lot of families with young kids, we go through frequent smoothie phases in our house. This leads to considerable morning experimentation with whichever fruits are ripe and on hand, often combined with yogurt and good raw local honey. When there's a glut of peaches sitting in the fruit bowl, here's our favorite thing to do with them.

MAKES 1 LARGE OR 2 SMALL SMOOTHIES

1 large banana, halved
1 medium peach, pitted (peeled if you like) and
    coarsely chopped
6 ounces Greek yogurt
¼ cup orange juice
1 teaspoon honey, preferably raw
1 cup small ice cubes
Mint sprigs, for garnish

In a large blender, combine all the ingredients except the mint. Blend until smooth and frothy, about 2 minutes. Serve immediately, garnished with fresh mint sprigs.

Chilled Peach and Blueberry Oatmeal

This recipe is a variation on traditional Swiss-style muesli, a cold breakfast cereal that is a crunchy, sweet, refreshing mélange ("muesli" means "mixture") of cereals, fruits, nuts, and dairy. It was originally developed as a health food by Swiss nutritionist Maximilian Bircher-Benner, history's first raw foods enthusiast, near the end of the nineteenth century. Since then, muesli has become a popular breakfast dish in Europe, where it's made with all manner of fruits and nuts. The precise inspiration for this recipe is a truly delicious version called Birchermüsli that I once sampled on the breakfast buffet at the Hotel des Balance in Lucerne.

MAKES 4 SERVINGS

2 cups Greek yogurt

2 cups old-fashioned rolled oats

1 cup peach nectar

1 cup almond milk

2 large peaches, peeled, pitted, and finely grated

1 cup fresh blueberries

3 tablespoons coarsely chopped almonds

1 tablespoon sunflower seeds

1 teaspoon cinnamon

⅓ cup whipped cream (optional)

In a large serving bowl, combine all the ingredients except the whipped cream and mix thoroughly. Cover the bowl tightly with plastic wrap and refrigerate overnight. If using whipped cream, fold in just before serving. Serve chilled.

Peach French Toast Sandwiches

This is a really decadent, messy, and fun brunch dish. If you're in the stage of life where "brunch" means the successful continuation of last night's date, you should make this. If you're in the stage of life where "brunch" means hanging out with toddlers who are watching cartoons while you try to read the New York Times, *you should make this too.*

MAKES 4 SERVINGS

4 tablespoons unsalted butter, divided
2 tablespoons light brown sugar
2 yellow peaches, pitted and cut into ½-inch cubes
2 tablespoons sour cream
8 slices white or sourdough bread, brioche, or challah
3 large eggs
½ teaspoon cinnamon
¾ cup heavy cream (optional)
Confectioners' sugar (optional)

Preheat the oven to 200°. In a large skillet over moderately low heat, melt 2 tablespoons of the butter until it foams. Add the brown sugar and stir to combine, about 30 seconds. Add the peaches, raise the heat to medium-high, and cook, stirring frequently, for 3 minutes. Stir in the sour cream and simmer for 2 minutes. Transfer the mixture to a bowl.

Place 4 slices of the bread on a work surface. Divide the peach mixture evenly among the slices, leaving about a ½-inch border on all sides. Top each with another slice of bread and press gently but firmly enough to hold the sandwich together.

In a shallow bowl, beat the eggs and cinnamon. Working in batches, soak the sandwiches in the egg mixture for 2 minutes per side.

Melt 1 tablespoon of the butter in a large skillet over medium heat. Fry 2 sandwiches until golden brown, 3–4 minutes per side. Transfer to a baking sheet and place in the oven to keep warm. Repeat with the remaining butter and sandwiches.

Beat the cream until soft peaks form. Halve each sandwich diagonally, sprinkle with confectioners' sugar, and top with whipped cream.

Peach Breakfast Parfait

My husband can't resist a yogurt parfait in a deli case, even at an airport snack bar. He says the combination of creamy yogurt, crunchy granola, and fresh fruit is irresistible. I'm a bacon-and-eggs person, but I like to be a good sport. In an effort to make a really good breakfast parfait, I learned to make granola. This is a very simple maple-walnut version. It makes more granola than you'll need for the parfaits, but that means you'll have a bunch of leftovers to play with and enjoy. In my opinion, the difference between a sad parfait and a really delicious one is the quality of the fruit. Slices of fresh ripe peaches (you can peel them if you like, but I never do) are really good with the tart, rich Greek yogurt. If you take the time to whisk the yogurt well with the vanilla and honey, it will develop a mousselike, airy consistency that really makes this dish.

MAKES 3 CUPS GRANOLA AND 2 PARFAITS

FOR THE GRANOLA

$2\frac{1}{2}$ cups thick-cut oats (not quick-cooking)
$\frac{1}{4}$ cup olive oil
$\frac{1}{4}$ cup maple syrup
$\frac{1}{2}$ teaspoon salt
$\frac{1}{2}$ teaspoon cinnamon
$\frac{1}{2}$ cup chopped walnuts

FOR THE PARFAITS

2 cups Greek yogurt (lowfat or nonfat is fine)
$\frac{1}{2}$ teaspoon vanilla
1 tablespoon honey
1 peach, pitted and sliced $\frac{1}{2}$-inch thick
$\frac{1}{2}$ cup granola

To make the granola, preheat the oven to 350°. Pour the oats into a shallow three-quart baking dish, then drizzle the olive oil and maple syrup over it. Sprinkle it with the salt and cinnamon. Bake for 5 minutes, then remove the dish from the oven and stir the mixture thoroughly. Return the dish to the oven and bake for 15 minutes more. Remove from the oven and stir in the walnuts. Bake until golden brown and toasty, about 5 minutes more. The granola can be stored in an airtight container for up to 2 weeks.

To make the parfaits, place two parfait glasses or glass ice cream bowls in the freezer (overnight or at least 15 minutes before you're planning to serve the parfaits). In a medium mixing bowl, whisk together the Greek yogurt, vanilla, and honey until thoroughly combined. The yogurt should loosen and become less dense.

Divide the yogurt evenly between the two parfait glasses. Top each with half of the peach slices, then ¼ cup of the granola. Serve immediately.

Spiced Peach Muffins

I learned about the King Arthur Flour Company, which was founded in 1790 and is based in Norwich, Vermont, when I went to work at Food & Wine *magazine in the summer of 1994. That was a few years before its products were distributed nationally and could be found in supermarkets everywhere, and I thought its flour was a revelation. I've used it ever since, and I rely on the company's website for a great selection of delicious baked goods. I've adapted these muffins from a version that originally appeared in the August 1991 issue of King Arthur Flour's newsletter,* The Baking Sheet. *I love the depth of the spices, especially the way they warm up and enhance the peaches' natural flavor. These are large, moist, cakey muffins. When it's not peach season, you can substitute 3 cups diced apples for the peaches for an autumnal treat.*

MAKES 16 MUFFINS

4½ cups all-purpose flour
1 teaspoon salt
4½ teaspoons baking powder
2 cups packed dark brown sugar
½ teaspoon allspice
1 teaspoon cardamom
1 teaspoon cinnamon
1 teaspoon peeled and finely grated fresh ginger
2 large eggs
¾ cup vegetable oil
1¼ cups milk
4 peaches, peeled, pitted, and diced
Granulated sugar

Preheat the oven to 400°. Grease 16 muffin cups.

In a large bowl, sift together the flour, salt, baking powder, brown sugar, and spices. Stir in the ginger, eggs, oil, and milk just to combine, taking care not to overmix the batter. Gently stir in the fruit. Mound equal amounts of the batter into the prepared cups; they should be very full. Sprinkle the top of each muffin with granulated sugar. Bake for 25–30 minutes or until a tester inserted into the center of the muffins comes out clean. Let the muffins cool in the pan for 5 minutes, then transfer them to a rack to cool for at least 15 minutes. Serve warm or at room temperature. Store in an airtight container.

Puffed Peach Omelet

The reason this custardy, fluffy peach "omelet" isn't a dessert is because it's both very light and not particularly sweet. What it is, though, is a traditional French preparation that's terrific for a romantic brunch à deux. It's a showstopper when you remove it from the oven, puffed and golden brown and demanding that you cut into it and eat it immediately. One omelet neatly serves two, but if you'd like to share the fun with a group, the best way is to make one omelet at a time and keep the finished omelets warming in a 300° oven while you continue to make as many as you need.

MAKES 2 SERVINGS

6 tablespoons plus ½ teaspoon granulated sugar, divided

1 teaspoon cinnamon

2 peaches, peeled, pitted, cored, and sliced ¼-inch thick

3 tablespoons plus 2 teaspoons unsalted butter, divided

4 large eggs, separated

1 teaspoon vanilla

1 tablespoon confectioners' sugar

Preheat the oven to 375°. In a large nonreactive bowl, mix ½ teaspoon of the granulated sugar with the cinnamon. Place the peaches in the bowl and toss to combine.

Heat 3 tablespoons of the butter in a small sauté pan over moderate heat. Add the peaches and sauté for about 5 minutes or until they begin to caramelize. Remove from the heat and set aside.

In a medium bowl using an electric mixer, beat the egg whites until stiff peaks form.

In a medium bowl using an electric mixer, beat the egg yolks with the remaining 6 tablespoons of granulated sugar until very light and fluffy. Fold in the vanilla. When well blended, fold in the beaten egg whites.

Melt the remaining 2 teaspoons of butter in an ovenproof omelet pan over moderate heat. Fan out the peaches in the pan and cover with the batter. Allow the omelet to begin to set, about 2 minutes. Place in the oven and bake for about 10 minutes or until puffed and golden. Remove from the oven and carefully invert onto a serving plate. Dust with confectioners' sugar, cut into wedges, and serve.

Appetizers, Salads, and Mains

I respect my friend Elaine Maisner immensely: She's a brilliant book editor at the University of North Carolina Press, she's a devoted wife and mother, and she's an accomplished home cook. When she and I discussed our plan for this book, one of the first things I said to her was, "I don't want to include any *stupid* recipes; you know what I mean?" I meant that I wanted to write and develop only recipes with peaches that make sense, not recipes for dishes with peaches tossed in (peach meatloaf, anyone? No thank you!). I probably spent more time thinking about the kinds of ways that the sweet freshness of peaches complements savory dishes, from light salads to roasted pork, than I did working on anything else. And I can promise you, there's not a single stupid recipe in the bunch.

Prosciutto-Wrapped Peaches, Easiest and Easy

Both of these preparations are—yes, simple—interpretations of the classic Italian prosciutto and melon appetizer, which likely originated in Parma, where the curing of hams is an ancient specialty. The point of it is to give guests (and yourself) something delicious to whet the palate or something to snack on with a nice glass of wine. You can wrap slices of ripe peach in salty, velvety prosciutto, or you can get a little fancy and grill the peach wedges first.

MAKES 8 SERVINGS

FOR THE EASIEST

4 peaches
4 ounces thinly sliced prosciutto (about 4 long slices)

Halve and pit the peaches, then cut each half lengthwise into thirds. You should have 24 wedges.

Tear the prosciutto lengthwise into 24 long strips. Wrap each strip around a peach wedge. Secure with toothpicks if you like.

4 peaches, quartered and pitted
1½ tablespoons olive oil
4 ounces thinly sliced prosciutto (about 4 long slices)
4 ounces crumbled feta cheese
16 basil leaves
Balsamic vinegar for drizzling (optional)

Preheat the grill to about 400°. Toss the peach quarters with the olive oil to coat. Oil the grill grates and grill the peaches until slightly tender and showing grill marks, about 2–3 minutes per side. Transfer to a platter until cool enough to handle.

Tear the prosciutto lengthwise into 16 long strips. Spread a small amount of the crumbled feta cheese on one side of each peach wedge, lay a basil leaf on top, and wrap with a strip of prosciutto. Secure with a toothpick if you like. Drizzle with a little balsamic vinegar, if using.

Peach Tempura

This is a really fun and unique appetizer inspired by the great Japanese tempura tradition. Tempura is one of the most common cooking techniques in Japan, and there are two competing theories as to its origins: one is that it was brought to Japan by Jesuit missionaries from Portugal in the sixteenth century, and the other is that it was introduced by the Chinese to Zen monks about 300 years ago. The idea behind it is to lightly, delicately enrobe food in a lacy fried coating to enhance its flavor and crunch. It's very easy and fun to make, and the peach wedges hold up very well to the light frying. You can make it as a fun summer appetizer with honey for dipping or with fresh greens drizzled with a Dijon vinaigrette, or you can serve the wedges atop vanilla or cinnamon ice cream for dessert.

MAKES 4 SERVINGS

4–6 cups rice bran oil

2 cups sweet rice flour (regular rice flour will work as well), divided

2 large egg whites

1 cup iced seltzer water or light beer

2 tablespoons granulated sugar

2 pounds slightly under-ripe peaches, cut into ¾-inch wedges

Confectioners' sugar (optional)

Honey (optional)

Pour the oil in a large, deep heavy-bottomed frying pan and heat to 350°.

While the oil is heating, in a medium mixing bowl, combine 1 cup of the rice flour with the egg whites, whisking slowly until the egg is absorbed. The mixture should be somewhat dry and lumpy.

Slowly add the seltzer water to the flour mixture, whisking constantly, until the batter is smooth and easy to stir. It should be thinner than pancake batter but still thick enough to coat the back of a spoon. Add the granulated sugar and mix gently.

Place the remaining 1 cup of rice flour on a shallow plate. Dredge the peach wedges in the rice flour, then dip them in the tempura batter. Using a slotted spoon, shake off the excess batter and transfer the peach wedges into the hot oil. Cook until the wedges are golden brown on all sides, about 2 minutes total.

Transfer to a rack until cool enough to handle. Serve the peach tempura slices warm, sprinkled with confectioners' sugar, with good local honey for dipping if you like.

Crook's Corner Green Peach Salad

The late southern chef and cooking teacher Bill Neal, founder of Crook's Corner restaurant in Chapel Hill, North Carolina, wrote one of my favorite books about southern cooking: Biscuits, Spoonbread, and Sweet Potato Pie *(originally published in 1990, available now in a reprinted edition). When I moved from New York City to Chapel Hill in 2004, I was naturally excited to visit the restaurant where he made his name. There I found an irresistibly friendly gang of food enthusiasts led by Neal's successor, chef Bill Smith. Smith has managed to weave Neal's specialties in with his own inspired take on southern staples. This green peach salad is an example of ingenuity at its finest. It answers the question of what to do with those stubborn peaches that won't ripen. Sprinkled with a little mint, sugar, salt, and good olive oil, they become a piquant and inviting summer salad, an ideal way to whet the appetite before whatever's about to come off the grill.*

MAKES 4–6 SERVINGS

2½ pounds unripe peaches, peeled, pitted, and
    sliced ¼-inch thick
Scant ¼ cup sugar
½ teaspoon salt
½ teaspoon freshly ground black pepper
2 tablespoons strong-flavored extra-virgin olive oil,
    like Greek or Lebanese
2 tablespoons fresh mint leaves, cut into very thin strips

In a large nonreactive bowl, toss the peach slices with the sugar and salt. Let rest for 5 minutes, then fold in the pepper, olive oil, and mint.

Chill, covered, in the refrigerator until ready to use. Serve within a few hours of preparation; if allowed to sit too long or overnight, the peaches will become mushy.

Tomato and Peach Salad with Feta and Red Onion

A lot of the peach recipes in this book will work with out-of-season or under-ripe peaches. But this unusual—and addictive—salad relies on the combination of two fruits that must be utterly ripe for the dish to be a success. Most people forget that tomatoes are actually a fruit, but when they're combined with peaches, that fact becomes incredibly obvious. The tomato's sweet tang is a lovely match for the juicy peach's flavor, and the feta and red onion cut through the fruit with creamy sharpness.

MAKES 4–6 SERVINGS

¼ cup thinly sliced red onion
1 pound peaches, peeled, pitted, and sliced ½-inch thick
1½ pounds best-quality tomatoes, such as homegrown
    heirlooms, of different sizes and colors, large ones diced
    and small ones halved
1 tablespoon red wine vinegar
3 tablespoons extra-virgin olive oil
1 teaspoon honey
Salt and freshly ground black pepper
4 ounces crumbled feta cheese
2 tablespoons small basil leaves or torn basil leaves

In a large bowl, combine the onion, peaches, and tomatoes.

In a medium bowl, whisk together the vinegar, olive oil, honey, and salt and pepper to taste. Drizzle over the fruit mixture, then add the feta and basil and gently toss. Serve immediately.

Arugula Salad with Grilled Peaches and Chicken

This is a great light dish, a refreshing lunch or dinner salad, or a good way to kick off a big meal. And it's very healthy and low in calories. You can easily change that by adding some feta or goat cheese, a handful of toasted cashews, or some crunchy, salty focaccia or sourdough croutons. Or you can keep it simple and feel very virtuous.

MAKES 4 FIRST-COURSE OR 2 ENTRÉE SERVINGS

1 pound boneless, skinless chicken breasts

Kosher salt and freshly ground black pepper

1 tablespoon olive oil, plus more for brushing

4 small peaches, halved and pitted

1 tablespoon Dijon mustard

1 tablespoon white wine vinegar

1 tablespoon water

8 cups baby arugula

Set a grill rack 4–6 inches above the heat source and heat the grill on high.

Season the chicken breasts with salt and pepper, then brush with olive oil. Grill the chicken, turning once, until it reaches an internal temperature of 165°, about 6–9 minutes on each side. Transfer the chicken to a cutting board, cover with aluminum foil, and let rest for 5 minutes.

Brush the peaches with olive oil and place skin-side up on the grill. Cook, turning once, until the peaches are juicy but not mushy, about 4 minutes per side. When the peaches are done, transfer to a plate.

In a salad bowl, whisk together the remaining 1 tablespoon olive oil, mustard, vinegar, and water. Toss with the arugula.

To serve, divide the arugula among 4 plates. Slice the chicken breasts and peaches and distribute evenly atop the dressed arugula.

Ginger-Peach Chicken

Ginger-Peach Chicken is one of those classic dinner-on-a-busy-weeknight dishes popularized during the casserole era of the late 1950s and 1960s, when many women were first going to work full-time. Most recipes for it consist of peach jelly mixed with dried ginger poured on top of skinless, boneless chicken breasts and then baked, which is uninspiring at best. This version maximizes the intense and delicious flavors of ginger and peach by employing fresh ginger and Asian accents like soy sauce and sesame oil. The recipe is also great for stubborn peaches that refuse to ripen because roasting softens their flesh and their tart flavor is welcome. In this more elaborate guise, which takes just a little more time and effort to prepare, Ginger-Peach Chicken becomes an even better dinner for a busy weeknight.

MAKES 4 SERVINGS

---

1 pound unripe, almost hard peaches, halved and pitted

2 red onions, halved and sliced ¼-inch thick

Kosher salt and freshly ground black pepper

2 tablespoons peeled and finely grated fresh ginger

2 tablespoons soy sauce

1 tablespoon plus 1 teaspoon vegetable oil, divided

1 tablespoon toasted sesame oil

½ teaspoon red pepper flakes

4 bone-in, skin-on chicken breasts

Steamed white or jasmine rice, for serving

Preheat the oven to 450°. Place the peaches and onions on a large rimmed baking sheet; season with salt and pepper. Sprinkle with the ginger, soy sauce, 1 tablespoon of the vegetable oil, sesame oil, and red pepper flakes; toss to coat.

Rub the chicken with the remaining 1 teaspoon vegetable oil and season with salt and pepper. Arrange the chicken skin-side up among the peaches and onions.

Roast until the chicken is opaque and registers 160° on an instant-read thermometer inserted in the thickest part of breast, 25–30 minutes. Serve the chicken with the peaches, onions, and rice.

Roasted Chicken
with Peaches and Rosemary

When I was growing up in a southern Jewish family, my grandmother made either barbecued chicken or pot roast (or both, depending on the size of the crowd) for our Shabbat dinner on Friday nights. Now that I'm a mother with my own household and Friday night dinners, roasted chicken has become my go-to dish; it's so easy to make, and even my pickiest eater likes it. I have a method I stick to for roasting the bird, but I often experiment with the flavors that surround it. For instance, I like the combination of peaches and shallots stuffed into the cavity. They are an especially sweet-yet-subtle, almost delicate accompaniment to the roasted chicken, and they make the house smell divinely warm and inviting while the chicken is cooking.

MAKES 4 SERVINGS

1 3½- to 4-pound whole chicken
2 tablespoons olive oil, divided
Salt and freshly ground black pepper
4 peaches, peeled (if desired), quartered, and pitted
4 small shallots, halved
1 tablespoon apple cider or red wine vinegar
6 sprigs fresh rosemary (optional)

Preheat the oven to 400°. Thoroughly pat the chicken dry with paper towels, rub with 1 tablespoon of the olive oil, and season liberally with salt and pepper. Place the bird in a roasting pan or baking dish.

In a small bowl, combine the remaining 1 tablespoon olive oil, peaches, shallots, and vinegar and salt and pepper to taste.

Fill the chicken cavity with the peach mixture, along with the rosemary sprigs, if using. Roast until the chicken is cooked through and a thigh registers 180° on a meat thermometer, about 65–75 minutes or until the juices from the cavity run clear without any pink and the chicken skin is browned and crisp. Remove the pan from the oven and let the chicken rest, covered loosely with foil, for 10 minutes before carving. Serve the chicken sliced, with the peaches, shallots, and pan jus spooned over it and good bread on the side.

Roasted Peach-Basil Chicken

"A man taking basil from a woman will love her always," opined
the Renaissance-era English politician and free-speech advocate
(and eventual Catholic martyr) Sir Thomas More. Basil is such
an interesting herb in part because its fragrance is so hard to pin
down; it can be sweet or savory and has assertive notes of licorice
and lemon but also an underlying subtlety. But I digress: What's
important here is that I once sampled some peach-basil ice cream,
and although I found that particular iteration weird, I believed
the combination had potential. What I arrived at was a peach-
basil sauce that makes an excellent glaze for roasted chicken, sweet
and tangy and incredibly perfumed of a summer garden.

MAKES 4 SERVINGS

---

1 3½- to 4-pound whole chicken
Salt and freshly ground black pepper
3 medium peaches, peeled, pitted, and cut into ½-inch cubes
3 tablespoons white wine vinegar
¼ cup tightly packed basil leaves
½ teaspoon salt
½ teaspoon freshly ground black pepper

Preheat the oven to 400°. Thoroughly pat the chicken dry with paper towels. Season liberally with salt and pepper.

In a medium saucepan, combine the peaches and vinegar. Over moderate heat cook until the peaches are tender, stirring often, about 5 minutes.

Pour the peaches and their liquid into a blender or food processor and purée until smooth. Add the basil and salt and pepper to taste. Process until smooth.

Gently loosen the skin of the chicken by sliding your fingers between the breast and skin and opening your fingers. Loosen as far as you can, down to the thighs and into the legs. Spoon half of the peach-basil glaze under the skin, and use your fingers to spread it evenly. With kitchen twine, tie the legs together tightly. Brush the remaining glaze evenly over the entire surface of the chicken. Place the chicken on the rack of a roasting pan and pour 1 cup water into the pan.

Roast until the chicken is cooked through and a thigh registers 180° on a meat thermometer, about 65–75 minutes or until the juices from the cavity run clear without any pink and the chicken skin is browned and crisp. Remove the pan from the oven and let the chicken rest, covered loosely with foil, for 10 minutes before carving. Serve the chicken sliced, with pan jus spooned over it, alongside egg noodles, mashed potatoes, or fluffy steamed rice.

Pork Tenderloin with Sage and Peach Sauce

This dish is adapted from a signature recipe of the Scotto family, who own a very chic Italian restaurant in Midtown Manhattan, Fresco by Scotto, and frequently appear in cooking segments on the Today *show. By all accounts, they're a loving clan who appreciate food that's rustic and hearty. This dish is a perfect example: The peach sauce and aromatic herbs add interest and excitement to the simply seared pork.*

MAKES 4–6 SERVINGS

2 cloves garlic, smashed

1 tablespoon chopped thyme

1 tablespoon chopped rosemary

2 tablespoons chopped sage

2 tablespoons kosher salt

1 tablespoon cracked black pepper

¼ cup extra-virgin olive oil, plus more for searing

3 tablespoons balsamic vinegar

1½–2 pounds pork tenderloin

3 cups peaches, pitted and cut into small cubes

½ cup sugar

Juice of 2 lemons

½ teaspoon fresh-cracked black pepper

1 cup chicken stock

¼ cup vermouth

¼ cup toasted slivered almonds (optional)

Mix together the garlic, herbs, salt, pepper, olive oil, and vinegar in a large bowl. Place the pork in the marinade, cover, and refrigerate for 2–6 hours.

Preheat the oven to 200°. Drizzle olive oil into a large skillet and heat over medium. Add the pork tenderloin and turn to brown evenly on all four sides, for an approximate cooking time of 10–12 minutes. Transfer the tenderloin to a baking pan, cover with foil, and keep warm in the oven until ready to serve.

In a medium skillet over moderately low heat, combine the peaches, sugar, lemon juice, pepper, and chicken stock. Cook over medium-low heat until the peaches just start to break apart, about 15–20 minutes. Add the vermouth and simmer until the sauce becomes shiny and thick. The peaches will fall apart to make their own sauce. Remove from the heat and fold in the almonds, if desired. To serve, slice the tenderloin on the bias ½-inch thick and serve topped with peach sauce.

Peach-Glazed Ham

The idea for this recipe came from one of my favorites in Saveur *magazine, where I worked as an editor from 2000 to 2006. Advertising executive Monte Mathews came up with the idea for a Christmas party ham basted with an orange marmalade–brown sugar glaze as a cheap and easy—yet festive—dish for a holiday buffet. When I moved to North Carolina, I adapted Mathews's wintery ham recipe for summer buffets and picnics by substituting a combination of peach nectar and fresh peaches for the marmalade. Serve the ham at room temperature surrounded by platters of sliced super-ripe tomatoes and other summer salads, and add plenty of good rolls or biscuits and nice mustards on the side.*

MAKES 10–12 DINNER OR UP TO 30 BUFFET SERVINGS

---

3 cups peach nectar

1 (1-inch) piece of fresh ginger, peeled and smashed

Juice of 1 lemon

4 cloves garlic, smashed

1 (14-pound) smoked ham

¼ cup Dijon mustard

1 cup packed light brown sugar

3 peaches, peeled, pitted, and sliced

Preheat the oven to 350°. In a medium saucepan, simmer the peach nectar, ginger, lemon juice, and garlic for 20 minutes. Strain the mixture into a bowl.

Place the ham in a roasting pan, coat it with the Dijon mustard, and sprinkle on the brown sugar. Pour the peach glaze into the pan and toss in the sliced peaches.

Bake the ham for 1½ hours, basting it every 15 minutes with the glaze from the bottom of the pan. When the ham is done, remove it from the oven and transfer it to a cutting board. Allow it to rest, covered with foil, for 30 minutes, then cut it into thin slices.

Wild Rice Salad with Peaches and Snap Peas

This is the perfect dish to bring to a potluck or picnic because it's colorful and inviting and it doesn't suffer for sitting at room temperature. Wild rice is earthy, toothsome, and crunchy, and the snap peas and almonds enhance those qualities. The peaches add softness and a lovely fresh, ripe essence, and the whole salad is gently bound together by the tart and creamy Greek yogurt.

MAKES 4–6 SIDE-DISH OR 10–12 BUFFET SERVINGS

1 cup raw wild rice
1 teaspoon salt plus more, to taste
½ cup Greek yogurt
2 tablespoons olive oil
¼ cup finely diced basil
Freshly ground black pepper
3 large peaches, peeled, pitted, and diced
½ pound sugar snap peas, cut diagonally into bite-size pieces
½ cup sliced almonds, lightly toasted

Rinse the wild rice in 2–3 changes of hot water, then drain. In a large stockpot over moderately high heat, bring 3 cups water to a boil. Add the rice and salt and return to a boil before reducing the heat to maintain a low simmer. Cover and cook until the rice is tender but not mushy, with some kernels puffed open, about 35–40 minutes. Drain the rice in a sieve or fine-mesh colander and set aside to cool, covered, for at least 1 hour.

In a large bowl, whisk together the yogurt, olive oil, basil, and salt and pepper to taste. Add the cooled rice, peaches, sugar snap peas, and almonds. Gently stir together and adjust the seasoning as desired. Cover and refrigerate for an hour or more before serving.

Grilled Lamb Chops with Peach-Parsley Chutney

Chutney is an Indian condiment used to accompany curries and tandori meat dishes. In the Indian canon, there are countless variations, including classic parsley and peach versions. The chutney here combines the best of both for a tart, sweet-and-sour tang that pairs beautifully with naturally gamy and earthy lamb. The generally woodsy and smoky nature of grilled foods is a great balance for this chutney, so feel free to serve it alongside grilled chicken breasts or use it to replace ketchup on grilled burgers for an exotic sweet-and-sour twist.

MAKES 4 SERVINGS

FOR THE LAMB

8 lamb loin chops, trimmed of fat

1/4 cup olive oil

2 tablespoons lemon juice or balsamic vinegar

Salt and freshly ground black pepper

FOR THE CHUTNEY

1 tablespoon olive oil

1 leek, white and tender green parts only, thinly sliced

2 peaches, peeled, pitted, and diced

2 tablespoons red wine vinegar

2 tablespoons light brown sugar

1/2 cup orange juice

1/4 cup minced parsley

To marinate the lamb, place the chops in a shallow glass or ceramic dish. Combine the olive oil and lemon juice or vinegar and pour into the dish, swirling the chops to coat both sides. Season to taste with salt and pepper, cover with plastic wrap, and marinate for 15–20 minutes.

To make the chutney, heat the olive oil in a large saucepan over medium heat. Add the leeks and cook for 2–3 minutes until softened. Add the peaches, vinegar, brown sugar, and orange juice to the pan, stir to combine, and bring to a boil. Reduce the heat to low and simmer until the peaches are soft and the mixture is syrupy, about 15–20 minutes. Pour into a bowl, stir in the parsley, cover with plastic wrap, and refrigerate until ready to serve.

Preheat a broiler or grill to medium high. Remove the lamb chops from the marinade and pat dry. Cook for 2–3 minutes on each side for medium rare. Serve topped with peach chutney alongside tabbouleh with warm pita bread triangles if you like.

Condiments

A condiment's job is to enhance the flavor of a dish it's served alongside without overpowering it. I learned this when I was working with the great professional barbecue cook Myron Mixon, with whom I co-wrote a barbecue cookbook. Mixon is constantly experimenting with his prize-winning sauce recipes—he's "the winningest man in barbecue," having won more national championships than any other competitor on the professional circuit—and he tinkers with his recipes all the time, keeping them fresh and new. He uses the sweetness of peaches in some of his sauces, and it gave me the idea to do the same, to see which condiments could benefit most from a subtle hint of the peach's natural sweetness.

Farmer's Daughter Brand
Classic Peach Preserves

Although I've been writing about food for twenty-odd years—but who's counting?—I don't much like to talk about the subject when I'm having downtime with my friends. That said, occasionally I meet someone professionally who is so devoted to the food they make or raise, whose work is so impressive, that I have no choice but to befriend that person. Such is the case with April McGreger, a self-taught former pastry chef based in Carrboro, North Carolina, who launched a business devoted to old-fashioned southern-style preserved foods. The daughter of a sweet potato farmer, McGreger was a graduate geology student who traveled to Italy and Japan to study volcanoes before she turned to food, and she brings a laser-like intensity to her work. I was wary of her serious demeanor for a long time, mistaking it for a lack of joy. When I got to know McGreger, I found her inspiration for preserves infectious—and joyful. I fell in love with her preserves, especially the peach and cherry varieties, and eventually she didn't have any choice but to be my friend; I wouldn't let up. This is her recipe for utterly iconic, chunky, sweet, and juicy southern peach preserves. She says: "The best peach preserves are made with perfectly ripe peaches and are cooked in very small batches. Resist the urge to double this recipe. Make a second batch instead."

MAKES 4 8-OUNCE JARS

3 pounds yellow peaches, peeled

2 pounds sugar

⅓ cup lemon juice

Cut the peaches in half over a large bowl and remove the pits. Cut each half into wedges about ½-inch thick. Combine the peach slices with the sugar and lemon juice in the bowl and mix well. Cover with plastic wrap and refrigerate overnight or for at least 4 hours.

The next day, sterilize 4 8-ounce canning jars and lids according to the manufacturer's directions. Place a small plate and three metal spoons in the freezer.

Transfer the peach mixture to a wide, nonreactive, heavy-bottomed pot and bring to a boil over high heat, stirring once to be sure all the sugar has dissolved. Cook for 5 minutes. Carefully skim the foam from the surface. If the preserves are foaming excessively, add 1 teaspoon unsalted butter. Return the mixture to a boil and cook until it registers 220° on a candy thermometer or for about 6–7 minutes more. As the mixture thickens, gently stir so it does not stick to the bottom of the pot and burn. Check the set of the preserves by scooping a little of the liquid with one of the frozen spoons and returning the spoon to the plate in the freezer. After 2 minutes, the jelly should be thick and hold its shape somewhat when you push it with your finger. If the jelly is still thin, boil the mixture for another minute and then test it again with another spoon. Be careful not to overcook the preserves since they will continue to set up as they cool.

Using a funnel, pour the preserves into the prepared sterilized jars. Fill each jar to the bottom of the funnel, about ¼-inch from the bottom of the jar threads. Wipe the jar rims with a moist paper towel and carefully position the lid on each jar. Screw the rings on tightly, and invert the jars on your countertop in order to properly seal them. After 5 minutes, flip the jars right side up and let cool for 24 hours undisturbed. Check the seals and refrigerate any jar whose lid pops up when pressed. Sealed jars can be stored for 1 year.

Pickled Peaches

In all likelihood, pickled peaches originated in the Deep South at the turn of the century as a strategy for what to do with a bumper crop of peaches or what the great writer Julia Reed once called "the tyranny of summer produce." If you're new to this sweet-and-sour condiment, you'll discover that it's an unusually refreshing and pucker-inducing treat. If you want the peaches sweet, swirl them into yogurt at breakfast or ice cream at dessert; if you want them savory, treat them as a condiment with country ham, roasted turkey, or — my favorite — fried chicken.

MAKES 3 PINTS

---

12 small peaches, peeled, each stuck with 2–4 cloves
1½ cups sugar
1 cup white vinegar
3 large cinnamon sticks (optional)

Cut a shallow X in the bottom of each peach with a sharp paring knife and blanch in 2 batches in a large pot of boiling water for 10–15 seconds. Transfer the peaches with a slotted spoon to a large bowl of ice water and let stand until cool enough to handle. Peel the peaches, then halve them lengthwise and pit. Toss the peaches with the sugar and chill, covered, for 8–12 hours.

Wash 3 pint jars, lids, and rings in hot soapy water, then rinse well. Put the jars on the rack of a canner and add enough water to cover them by 2 inches. Boil, covered, for 10 minutes. Cover the lids with water in a small saucepan and heat, covered, until a thermometer registers 180° (do not let boil). Keep the jars and lids submerged in hot water, covered, until ready to use.

In a large nonreactive stockpot, mix the vinegar and cinnamon sticks, if desired, with the peaches and their accumulated juices. Bring to a boil over moderate heat, skimming off the foam. Reduce the heat and simmer until the peaches are barely tender, about 3 minutes.

Remove the jars and lids from the water, reserving the water in the canner, and transfer to a clean kitchen towel to dry them. Then divide the peaches and cinnamon sticks among the jars using a slotted spoon. Return the peach-cooking liquid to a boil, then pour into the jars, leaving ¼ inch of space at the top. Run a thin knife between the peaches and the sides of jars to eliminate air bubbles.

Wipe off the rims of the filled jars with a damp kitchen towel, place the lids on the jars, then firmly screw on the rings. Put the sealed jars on the rack of the canner and, if necessary, add enough hot water to cover the jars by 2 inches. Boil the jars for 20 minutes, covered, then transfer with tongs to a towel-lined surface to cool. The jars will seal as they cool (a ping signals that the vacuum that forms at the top of the jar has made the lid concave). After the jars have cooled for 12–24 hours, press the center of each lid to check that it's concave, then remove the ring and try to lift off the lid with your fingertips. If you can't, the lid has a good seal. Store in a cool dry place for up to 1 year. Place any jars that haven't sealed in the refrigerator and use them first.

Tangy Peach Barbecue Sauce

One of the most unique people I've ever encountered in my years as a food reporter is Myron Mixon. Mixon is from Unadilla, Georgia, and has won more championships and more money on the professional barbecuing circuit than any other living person, taking home roomfuls of trophies and over a million dollars in prizes. *This recipe is an adaptation of a type of sauce I happened upon when I was working with Mixon on his cookbook* Smokin' with Myron Mixon. *Serious barbecue guys are always messing with their secret formulas for sauces and rubs.*

MAKES ABOUT 2 ½ CUPS

---

2 tablespoons olive oil

1 small red onion, thinly sliced

3 peaches, pitted, cut into ¼-inch cubes

2 tablespoons peeled and minced fresh ginger

2 medium ripe tomatoes, cut into ¼-inch cubes

½ cup cider vinegar

½ cup orange juice

⅓ cup packed light brown sugar

1 teaspoon cardamom

Salt and freshly ground black pepper

In a large skillet over medium-high heat, heat the olive oil until hot but not smoking. Add the onions and cook, stirring occasionally, until golden brown, about 12 minutes.

Add the peaches, ginger, and tomatoes and cook, stirring frequently, about 2 minutes. Stir in the vinegar, orange juice, brown sugar, cardamom, and salt and pepper to taste. Bring the mixture to a boil, then lower the heat and simmer until reduced by about half and thickened slightly, about 20 minutes. Adjust the seasoning.

Transfer the sauce to a blender or food processor and purée until smooth. Serve immediately or allow to cool completely and then store covered in the refrigerator for up to 1 month.

Watermelon-Peach Chutney

This chutney is a fusion of Indian tradition and southern summer flavors. I once got to meet the legendary Indian cooking teacher—and British soap opera actress!—Madhur Jaffrey, whose regal demeanor left an impression on me. Jaffrey doesn't just create great authentic Indian recipes; she's also fabulous. This recipe is inspired by one for Delhi-style peach chutney in her book World Vegetarian. *I've augmented the recipe with watermelon and made it more Western by toning down the spices. If you'd like to make it more Indian, you can add a dash or two of cumin, mustard seed, and fennel seed and serve it with pappadums, as Jaffrey does. If you'd like to make it more southern, which is what I do, you can serve it with fried chicken and biscuits.*

MAKES ABOUT 1 ½ CUPS

---

1 tablespoon olive oil
2 large peaches, peeled, pitted, and finely chopped
1 (1-inch) piece of fresh ginger, peeled and finely grated
2 tablespoons red wine vinegar
2 tablespoons light brown sugar
½ cup seeded, chopped watermelon
4 scallions, white and tender green parts, finely chopped

Combine all the ingredients in a heavy nonreactive pan over moderately high heat and bring to a boil. Reduce the heat to medium-low and cook at a vigorous simmer for about 30 minutes or until the chutney has a thick, jam-like consistency. Stir frequently and turn the heat down slightly to prevent the chutney from sticking to the bottom of the pan.

Once the chutney has thickened, remove it from the heat and cool completely. It will thicken more as it cools. Pour the chutney into a clean jar and cover it with a nonmetallic lid. Store in a cool place in the refrigerator.

Mango-Peach Salsa

Obviously inspired by the Mexican flavors of traditional tomato, onion, and cilantro-spiked salsa, this fruity version is also authentic to Mexico. Mexico has the kind of tropical climate that fruits like mangos and peaches love, and when they're in season, lots of home cooks use the sweet fruits in a salsa that's spicy, tangy, and sweet in equal measure. It's marvelous on fish tacos, with Tex-Mex fajitas, and on its own with freshly fried (or even store-bought) tortilla chips.

MAKES 12 SERVINGS

1½ cups chopped tomatoes
¾ cup peeled, pitted, and chopped peaches
½ cup chopped red onion
½ cup chopped yellow pepper
½ cup peeled, chopped mango
2 tablespoons seeded, chopped jalapeño
3 garlic cloves, minced
1½ teaspoons lime juice
½ teaspoon minced cilantro
Kosher salt
Tortilla or plantain chips, for serving

In a large nonreactive bowl, combine all the ingredients except salt and stir gently. Add salt to taste. Cover and refrigerate for at least 2 hours before serving. Serve with tortilla or plantain chips.

Honey-Peach Butter

The funny thing about a fruit butter is that it's not actually butter. *It's a condiment made by gently slow-cooking puréed fruit with sugar and spices. The hallmark of a good fruit butter is its thickness—fruit butters are made for spreading on toast and other favorite breads. I love experimenting with ways to sweeten fruit without sugar. Although this recipe includes white sugar, a lot of its sweetness and warmth comes from the flavor of honey, so buy the best local raw honey you can find—it adds depth to the peaches. This is marvelous on an English muffin with a cup of hot tea for breakfast or as a snack during a summer rain shower. For a variation, you can add a sprig or two of rosemary to the pot for a more aromatic butter, then remove it before storing the butter.*

MAKES 2–4 8-OUNCE JARS

9 peaches, peeled, pitted, and sliced
¼ cup water
1 cup sugar
¼ cup honey

In a large, heavy pot or Dutch oven, combine the peaches and water. Over moderately high heat, bring to a boil and reduce the heat to low. Simmer, covered, for 10–15 minutes or until the peaches are tender but not falling apart. Remove from the heat and cool slightly.

Using a blender or food processor, purée the peaches until perfectly smooth. Return the peach purée to the pot and add the sugar and honey. Over moderate heat, bring to a boil, stirring constantly to dissolve the sugar. When the sugar is dissolved, reduce the heat to low and simmer, uncovered, stirring frequently, for about 15 minutes or until the mixture is thick and mounds on a spoon.

Let cool and ladle into a container. Store airtight in the refrigerator for up to 2 weeks.

Drinks

On a really hot day, there's nothing better than sipping an icy peach-spiked concoction—preferably on an island, in a hammock, before a vast cloudless horizon and a gleaming ocean. Let's face it, though—we're seldom, if ever, enmeshed in such a scenario. But we can still drink a peachy drink and dream, can't we? That's the most important part of the fantasy and, coincidentally, the easiest one to make happen. Peaches are an ideal natural sweetener for cocktails, a bartender's secret weapon.

The Southern Neighbor Cocktail

If you have a favorite bartender, you know the value of a guy (or girl) who can make your favorite drink and serve it up with some quality banter on the side. I have such a bartender: the great Gary Crunkleton, whose bar, The Crunkleton, lines the main drag of my hometown, Chapel Hill, North Carolina. Everything about him is larger-than-life, especially his sense of humor. Crunkleton (the name's Scottish) has made a study of mixology and loves to create new cocktails. One of his signature drinks is called the Southern Neighbor, because "it could turn anyone friendly." It's made with Damiana, a subtly fig-flavored herbal liqueur from Mexico, which is available in good liquor stores.

MAKES 4 COCKTAILS

½ cup sugar
¼ cup water
2 very ripe, soft peaches, peeled, pitted, and thinly sliced
4 ounces apple brandy
4 ounces gin
4 ounces Damiana
2 ounces lemon juice
4 mint sprigs, for garnish

Place the sugar and water in a large saucepan over medium heat and stir until the sugar dissolves, about 5 minutes. Cool completely.

In a large tumbler, mash the peaches gently with the back of a spoon until the fruit releases its juices.

Combine the peaches, brandy, gin, Damiana, and lemon juice in a large shaker along with a few ice cubes. Shake well. Strain into 4 Collins glasses filled with ice. Garnish each with a fresh mint sprig.

Peach Iced Tea

This is a peach-touched version of the Arnold Palmer, the combination of lemonade and iced tea popularized by the golf legend. "The idea for the combination struck me after a round of golf in the [California] desert in the early '60s. I wanted something that would be refreshing and realized that lemonade would be a natural complement to iced tea, since most people add a lemon wedge to their tea. When I first started ordering the combination in Palm Springs, a sharp waitress . . . started calling it an Arnold Palmer," Palmer told Saveur *magazine in 2004. Palmer is many things, but a southerner he is not; if he were, he'd surely have put slices of ripe peaches in his iced tea, as is customary anywhere peaches are grown and iced tea is consumed. This version combines puréed fresh peaches with homemade iced tea. For a special "adult" beverage, you can spike each glass with a shot of vodka; in golf circles, when an Arnold Palmer is spiked with vodka, it's called a John Daly.*

MAKES 1 GALLON

4 cups water, divided
3 family-size tea bags
2 peaches, peeled, pitted, and sliced
½ cup sugar

In a large pot over high heat, bring 3 cups of the water to a rolling boil. Remove from the heat. Add the tea bags, cover, and steep for 15 minutes. Meanwhile, place the peaches and the remaining 1 cup of water in a blender and blend until very smooth, at least 3 minutes. Pour the peach mixture, tea, and sugar into a 1 gallon pitcher. Fill the pitcher to the top with water, and stir until blended.

Peach-Blackberry Soda

Although I was born and raised in Atlanta, a big part of my heart is in New York City, where my career grew up, if you will. Of the many guilty pleasures I picked up in the Big Apple, an intense love of seltzer is probably the biggest; the slight mineral flavor is so refreshing that I've become an addict. I am always experimenting with different seltzer flavors, which is how this soda came about.

To make a more adult version of this soda, add a shot of ice-cold vodka to each glass and garnish with a couple of fresh mint leaves.

MAKES 4 DRINKS

---

2 cups water

1 cup sugar

2 peaches, peeled, pitted, and sliced ½-inch thick

1 cup fresh or frozen blackberries

¼ cup lemon juice

1 teaspoon lemon zest

1 cup sparkling water

In a small saucepan, bring the water and sugar to a boil over medium-high heat, stirring constantly until the sugar has dissolved, 2–3 minutes. Set aside to cool for 20 minutes.

In a blender, combine the cooled syrup, peaches, blackberries, lemon juice, and lemon zest. Blend until smooth. Add the sparkling water and pour into an ice-filled pitcher. Serve immediately.

Classic Bellini Cocktail

The Bellini, a deceptively simple cocktail of peach purée with sparkling wine, was created in the legendary Harry's Bar in Venice, Italy, which was opened in 1931 by Giuseppe Cipriani, a former hotel waiter. Harry's Bar has become one of the world's most lauded, and expensive, upper-class oases, and along the way, it also became famous for its dressed-up versions of homey Italian specialties and its signature carpaccio appetizer. The magic of its signature cocktail, named for Italian opera composer Vincenzo Bellini, is in the combination of very ripe fruit with very cold, crisp bubbly. Which means it's very good on a hot day. Or any day, for that matter.

MAKES 6 COCKTAILS

1 cup sugar

½ cup water

½ pound peaches, peeled, pitted, and sliced

1 teaspoon grated orange peel

1–2 (750 ml) bottles prosecco or other sparkling wine, chilled

Fresh strawberries, raspberries, and blueberries, for garnish

Orange peel twists, for garnish

Place the sugar and water in a large saucepan over medium heat and stir until the sugar dissolves, about 5 minutes. Cool completely.

Purée the peaches and grated orange peel in a blender with ½ cup of the sugar syrup until smooth, at least 3 minutes. Strain through a fine-mesh strainer into a bowl. Cover and refrigerate.

For each serving, place 2–4 tablespoons of fruit purée into a champagne flute. Slowly pour enough prosecco into the flute to fill it. Gently stir to blend. Garnish with whole berries and orange peel twists.

Peach Sangria

Sangria is the Spanish punch traditionally made with red wine ("sangria" means "bleeding") diluted with a little sugar and orange juice and sweetened with nutmeg; sliced lemons and oranges are added to macerate, and then still or sparkling water is added when the drink is served. It first caught the attention of Americans when it was served in the Spanish pavilion of the 1964 New York World's Fair. Americans took the drink into their own hands, adding all sorts of fruits, including chopped apples, cherries, and mangoes. Known as white sangria, this laidback version of the drink is made with Spanish white wine and peaches, and it's a huge crowd pleaser. It's best made a few hours in advance and chilled until ready to serve.

MAKES 4–6 COCKTAILS

¼ cup sugar

½ cup water, divided

2 peaches, peeled, halved, and pitted

1 (750 ml) bottle white Spanish table wine, such as
    Albariño, Viura, or Verdejo

3 ounces brandy

1 cup orange juice

1 cup pineapple juice

Fresh peaches, oranges, and apples, diced (optional)

In a small nonreactive saucepan over moderately high heat, combine the sugar and ¼ cup of the water and bring to a boil. Boil for 2 minutes, stirring constantly to dissolve the sugar, then remove from the heat and let cool.

In a blender, combine the peaches with the remaining ¼ cup of water and purée until smooth, at least 3 minutes. Strain and reserve the purée.

Pour the remaining ingredients in a large pitcher along with the simple syrup and peach purée. Stir in the diced fruits, if using. Refrigerate the pitcher, covered, 8–48 hours. Serve over ice.

Frozen White Peach Margarita

If you associate flavored frozen margaritas with college girls gone wild in Cancun, I present this white peach–silver tequila version, which is a refreshing, chunky-fruity, smoothie-like beverage especially made for a hot day or some hot and spicy Mexican food. The peach schnapps is included mostly for its peachy fragrance and sweetness, but if you find it too cloying—or collegiate—then simply omit it.

MAKES 2 COCKTAILS

1 large white peach, pitted
½ cup water
Ice
3 ounces silver tequila
Juice of 1 lime
1½ ounces peach schnapps (optional)

In a blender, combine the peach and water. Blend until completely smooth, at least 3 minutes. Strain the purée to get rid of the pulp if you like; if you prefer it thicker, don't bother. Add ice to fill the blender three-quarters of the way to the top. Add the rest of the ingredients and blend. Serve immediately, ice-cold.

Vin de Pêche à la Alice Waters

Alice Waters, who has owned and operated Chez Panisse restaurant in Berkeley, California, for more than thirty years, is a leading advocate of the "eat local" food movement. As such, she's always on the frontlines of U.S. food politics. She has testified before Congress many times on subjects like fast food in public schools (she's against it), and she pioneered the "Edible Schoolyard" movement to help inner-city kids build gardens. She's also a tremendous lover of peaches. "Even amid the abundance of other summertime fruits, peaches are our favorite for dessert," she wrote in Chez Panisse Fruits. *At Chez Panisse, a specialty of the house in the summer is a Provençal-style* vin de pêche, *a refreshing yet sweet aperitif that derives its subtle flavor from the tender peach leaves of early summer. How can you get peach leaves? Peaches are all over farmers' markets in the summer, and most farmers are happy to sell the otherwise useless leaves. You can also get dried peach leaves from any good herbalist or vitamin shop or online from a reputable botanical company; the dried leaves can be easily reconstituted in warm water.*

MAKES ABOUT 6 CUPS

---

120 peach leaves, picked in late spring or early summer, washed and dried
1 (750 ml) bottle red wine (preferably a light, fruity Zinfandel)
½ cup cognac
2 cups sugar

Combine all the ingredients in a nonreactive container and cover tightly. Store in a cool, dark cellar or in the refrigerator for 30 days. Strain out the leaves and pour the liquid into a clean wine bottle. Serve as an aperitif, well chilled or over ice.

Index